PARALLEL UNIVERSES

ALSO BY ROZ CHAST:

Last Resorts

Unscientific Americans

PARALLEL UNIVERSES

cartoons by Roz Chast

HARPER & ROW, PUBLISHERS, New York
Cambridge, Philadelphia, San Francisco, London,
Mexico City, São Paulo, Singapore, Sydney

1817

For Bill

Of the 131 drawings in Parallel Universes, 71 originally appeared in The New Yorker (Copyright © 1979, 1980, 1981, 1982, 1983, 1984 by The New Yorker Magazine, Inc.). Grateful acknowledgment is made to The New Yorker for permission to reprint.

Several cartoons have also appeared in Mother Jones, National Lampoon, Psychology Today and Horticulture.

Designer : Francesca Belanger

LIBRARY OF CONGRESS CATALOGING IN PUBLICATION DATA

Chast, Roz
    Parallel universes.

    1. American wit and humor, Pictorial. I. Title.
NC1429.C525A4 1984   741.5'973   84-47563
ISBN 0-06-091177-8 (pbk.)

    85 86 87 88 10 9 8 7 6 5 4 3

FUN   BOB   BORING

fig. 1·A

R Chast

JOE'S FAVORITE CHAIR
TURNS OVER

Thanks to Re-Education...

The Wicked Witch of the East ~ NOW A DIETITIAN AT THE PARKVILLE SCHOOL

Cinderella's Stepsisters ~ ALL WORKING IN N.Y.C.'S GARMENT DISTRICT

The Big, Bad Wolf ~ OWNS GALLERY WHICH HANDLES ANIMAL ART ONLY

R. Chast

GRANTS & RECIPIENTS

$25,000 from the Lucy and Ed Flanders Foundation for Going to Bed on Time

$40,000 from the Lucy Flanders Institute for Taking Care of Barky

$75,000 from the Ed Flanders Society for Growing Up Without Becoming Too Much of a Jerk

R. Chast

Oh? So our ICED TEA isn't quite GOOD ENOUGH for you, Mrs. Widmark?
I'm not so sure if someone who is on the verge of bankruptcy DESERVES pie, Mr. Evanston.
I'm sorry, Miss Driscoll. If you don't finish your greens, you don't get your coffee. House rules.
Sally & Joe's
FAMILY · STYLE RESTAURANT
R. Chast

GREGOR S.'s FURTHER ADVENTURES

Well, in this version, the Cockroach Man doesn't die.

He gets really ticked off at his family and runs away.

SUITCASES →

Good-bye, you chowder-heads!

Down the street is a circus which he finds interesting.

COTTO CAN

25¢

He becomes part of this Human Insect Exhibit.

See ~ THE FLY MAN COME INSIDE →

See ~ THE ANT MAN COME INSIDE →

See ~ THE COCK-ROACH MAN COME INSIDE →

Their case histories were remarkably similar to Gregor's.

Yeah— I remember— one day I woke up and I was an ant!

They all got to be real close.

I'm on in 5 minutes.

R. Chast

The Tabletop Family

They make their home on a tabletop,
where fun and laughter never stop.
They're smart and nice and very cute,
much better than a bowl of fruit.

R. Chast

THE LADY OR THE TIGER OR THE CLOSET?

R. Chast

CRUISES TO NOWHERE

A visit with Aunt Zelda

A tête-à-tête with Mathilda

A luncheon date with Victor

R. Chast

THE MYSTERY OF THINGS

Who knows?

One day your hair dryer works just fine—

VRRRR

the next day it's sending out sparks to beat the band.

Who knows?

R. Chast

Dentists in Space, CHAPTER 1

It was just the old bunch of guys:

Eric Harry Jay Stan

Come summer, they would take these fishing trips together, year after year.
> Hey, you guys, ready to go up to Lake Winnebasko?

It was always the same thing. They'd take Stan's canoe, and camp along the banks of Lake Winnebasko for about a week, and then come home, covered with mosquito bites.

CALOMINE

Well, this year was different. Jay's brother-in-law was working at NASA, and one day he asked Jay if he'd like to be the dentist aboard the Columbia CXXI.

Jay agreed, if they allowed him to bring along the rest of the guys.

It was all arranged. It was just like their old canoe trips, with two differences:

① DIFFERENT GEAR

and ② INSTEAD OF A WEEK, IT WAS 6 MONTHS. The wives were aggrieved and wanted to come along.

But that's another story.
> Well, what do you think we ought to do?

R Chast

AFTERNOON OF THE LIVING DEAD

R. Chast

KOANS for LANDLORDS

If the ceiling caves in, does it matter in China?

What is the sound of one radiator breaking?

Do the walls care if they are co-op or rental?

APARTMENT 6-J:
LAST BASTION OF EUCLIDITY

R. Chast

"*I'll make a deal with you. You don't push my buttons,
and I won't pull your strings.*"

RECIPES
from the
AMERICAN CHEESE COUNCIL

Cheese Omelette

2 eggs
5 lb. Swiss cheese
1 tbsp. butter

Melt butter in pan. Add eggs and cheese. Cook until done. Serves 2.

Cheese Salad

1 tomato	1 lb. feta cheese
1 mushroom	1 lb. blue cheese
1 leaf of lettuce	1 lb. Parmesan
2 lb. cheddar	½ lb. Camembert
1 lb. Muenster	½ lb. Gruyère

Make everything bite-sized, then place in bowl. Serves 6 cheese-loving people.

Cheese Patties

6 lb. soft cheese

Form cheese into patties. Serve on a bun. Makes enough for 12 patties.

Cheese Pick-Me-Up

½ cup water
1 lb. Brie

Put everything in blender at a high speed. Serve immediately. Just enough for one.

R Chast

LITE® BOOKS

Madame Bovary LITE®

Madame B., dissatisfied with her lot in life, goes on a shopping spree. Later, she returns everything but a hat.

Anna Karenina LITE®

Anna K., a married woman, has a date with a Count Vronsky. He moves away, and they never see each other again.

Crime and Punishment LITE®

Raskolnikov writes a nasty letter to a pawn-broker, but later feels guilty and apologizes.

R. Chast

MIX 'N' MATCH

R. Chast

MEDICAL MILE

Dental Hut

DENTAL HUT

DRIVE-THRU

Brain Surgery 'n' Brew

WAITING ROOM

Check-up King

CHECK-UP KING
ENTRANCE   EXIT

R. Chast

MIKE'S LIFE

Mike's life was made up of a succession of endlessly repeating days—

—each exactly like the one before and after it.

19 20 21 22 23

Hummmm....

It was a humdrum existence, but he didn't mind.

6 o'clock— time for macaroni and cheese

He was no bohemian, that's for sure!

his cousin

R. Chast

CENTERVILLE
SAVINGS & LOAN

Deposit $10.⁰⁰ for 2³/₄ years and choose from the following items:

Deposit $50.⁰⁰ for 7¹/₄ years and receive your choice of:

pack of gum

box of reinforcements

pair of socks

comb and pocket mirror

thank-you call from Shirley Veedle

Deposit $100.⁰⁰ for 11¹/₂ years and select one of these items as a bonus:

thank-you note from Shirley Veedle

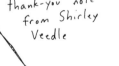

lunch for two at the Château Centerville

adhesive assortment-pak

thank-you letter from Shirley Veedle

R. Chast

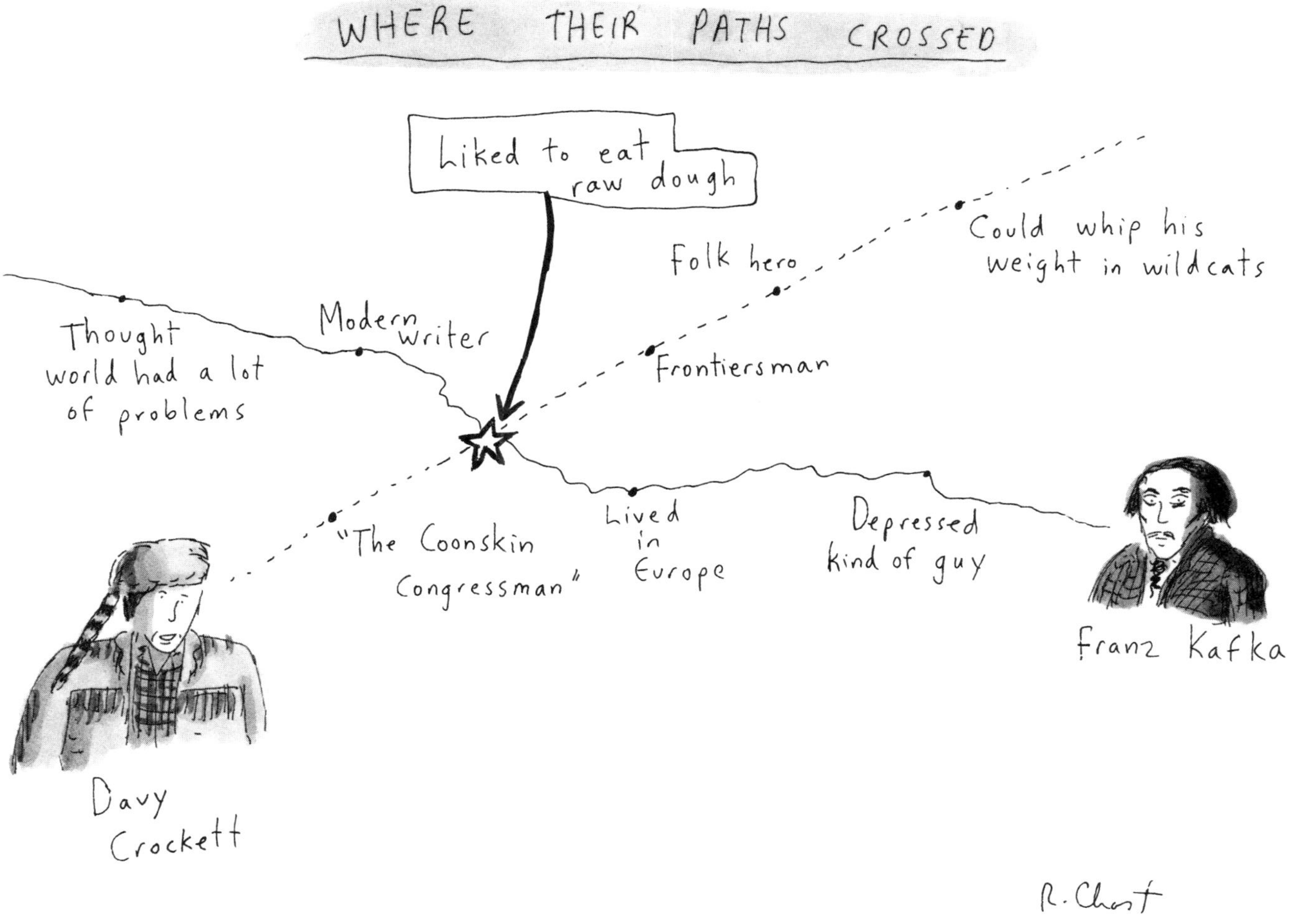

WHERE THEIR PATHS CROSSED

Liked to eat raw dough

Could whip his weight in wildcats

Folk hero

Modern writer

Thought world had a lot of problems

Frontiersman

"The Coonskin Congressman"

Lived in Europe

Depressed kind of guy

Davy Crockett

Franz Kafka

R. Chast

FALSE STARTS

It all began with a shoe,

and a cup and saucer.

It all began with a shoe,

and the three Jones children,

It began with an old book with a green cover.

A red cover.

Roz Chast

HOG HEAVEN

Hot-and-cold running mud

Unlimited corn

No Farmer Joe

R. Chast

CHICK'N-in-a-THIMBLE
THE RESTAURANT FOR PEOPLE WHO EAT LIKE BIRDS!

1/4 chicken	$3.95	
1/8 chicken	$2.49	
1/16 chicken	$1.49	
1/32 chicken	$.99	
1/64 chicken	$.59	
1/128 chicken	$.39	
1/256 chicken	$.29	
1/512 chicken	$.19	
1/1,024 chicken	$.13	
1/2,048 chicken	$.09	
1/4,096 chicken	$.06	
1/8,192 chicken	$.04	

P. Chast

MOMS OF OTHER PLANETS

R. Chast

HYPOCHONDRIA
CARDS

4 HYPO-ALLERGENIC CARDS IN EACH HERMETICALLY
SEALED PACKET, PLUS 1 STICK VERY ORGANIC GUM

#93- BENGALI FOOT
FEVER ~
Foot itches; cough;
mood change.

#104- GEEBLER'S
SYNDROME ~
Queasiness; hands feel
overly warm.

#216- TURVEY'S
DISEASE ~
Strange taste in mouth;
joints ache.

#275- HARNIK'S
CONDITION -
Memory lapse; arm hurts
when pinched a certain
way.

R. Chast

BUZZWORDS
OF
NORTH 7th STREET

Trip Memory Test

Who are these people?

Name the restaurant Uncle Martin brought everybody to.

Menu

You had an entire conversation with this person about: (CHECK ONE)
a) the space program
b) what he did last summer
c) Shogun

R. Chast

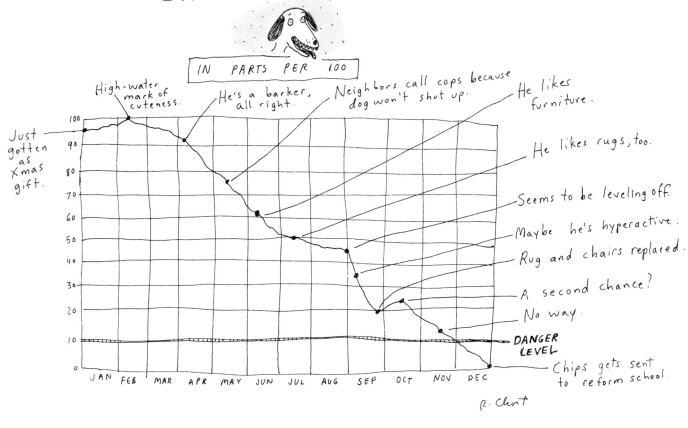

CHIPS' CUTENESS GRAPH

IN PARTS PER 100

High-water mark of cuteness.

He's a barker, all right.

Neighbors call cops because dog won't shut up.

He likes furniture.

Just gotten as Xmas gift.

He likes rugs, too.

Seems to be leveling off.

Maybe he's hyperactive.

Rug and chairs replaced.

A second chance?

No way.

DANGER LEVEL

Chips gets sent to reform school.

JAN FEB MAR APR MAY JUN JUL AUG SEP OCT NOV DEC

R. Chast

NEW CULTIVARS

Hudson Valley Behemoths

Stacking Red Bonnies

Saffron Delights

Northern Teeny-tinies

Smooth-skinned Tiptops

Babs' Inedible Beauties

R. Chast

The Cereal's Universe

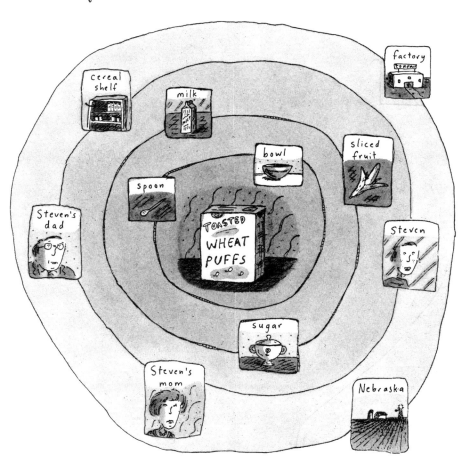

PORTENTS OF AUNT VERNA

Cat runs away.

Anybody seen Snuffy?

"High, Wide, and Handsome" shows up on TV.

Cloud shaped like her head passes over.

R. Chast

FROM HERE ...... TO ETERNITY

A living room somewhere
in the Wheat Belt

Math class

The Shopaway,
Route 89

The checkout
line

A bus stop on
Baines Avenue

A visit with
Ezra

R. Chast

SMITH, SMITH, SMITH, SMITH & SMITHEREENS

THE BREAKDOWN

CLOUD 9

Cruise around world on luxury liner for two months.

CLOUD 6

Three weeks in Paris.

CLOUD 3

Five days in Miami.

CLOUD 1

Weekend in Akron.

R. Chast

Mistaken Impressions

Oh, I thought you were a historical landmark!

I COULD'VE SWORN you were some leftover osso buco!

I must've mixed you up with my broken blow-dryer!

R. Chast

STANDING ROOM ONLY

This play

TWO MINUTES TO FUN

This bus

BOB'S PHARMACY

CENTRAL AVE.

This apartment

3-N

WELCOME

R. Chast

THE VELCROS AT HOME

ANSWERS TO
LAST WEEK'S PUZZLE

"A TOUGHIE"

R·Chast

The Three Certainties

DEATH

TAXES

BOBO

R. Chast

The Imperfect Hostess

WHAT GOES WITH WHAT?

Pencils

Worms

Flannel

Gravel

Telephone wire

Typewriter ribbon

Chablis

Light Burgundy

Soave

Ale

Champagne

Dry sherry

R. Chast

Superheroes

Stands up to the wear and tear of everyday life!

Doesn't let little things get to him!

Still likes people even after living in New York for several years!

R. Chast

LIFE GETS LUSH

It started out small... A little extra here, a nice thing there.

Say! That's exactly the tie I've been looking for!

Not too alarming. Just odd.

Oh! Excuse me

BONK

What did it mean when his super actually fixed his sink the same day it stopped up??!

I'll be done in a jiffy!

He tried to tip him $5.00, but to no avail!

Shucks! You just gave me a bunch of money at Christmas!

As if by magic, all the crazies in his life stopped calling.

Oh, no... I bet it's Louie....

R-R-RING

Suddenly, he had friends he never knew he had.

Hi! This is Bonnie. We met at a party last week. Would you like to come to the party? My dad has a big YACHT, and lots of fun, so...

What had happened?! Had he sold his soul to the devil in his SLEEP ???

Here ya go! It's all yours!

Even the guy at the bakery was in on it...

Let's see... It totals up to $7.89 - just give me three bucks.

Bonnie's party was not the hideous humiliation he had imagined it would be.

That guy is such a loser!

Mr. Middle Class!

Yeah! Who invited him?

Instead, he had had a very nice time.

Where did you come up with all that data on used furniture?

Life went on like this for a good six weeks.

Then, suddenly...

Hi, this is Louie. Listen, I think my dog just ate my stamp collection. Oh, ha, ha, they were under the sink. Can you loan me $500? The city towed my car to New and the den for root canal surgery

R. Chast

LOSS LEADERS

THEY CHANGED THEIR TUNES

From "Oh! Susanna" to "Edelweiss."

From "The Moonlight Sonata" to "The Flight of the Bumblebee."

From "Goldfinger" to "Jingle Bells."

R. Chast

THE STYLE OF ELEMENTS

Sure, they're tiny!

But that doesn't mean they have no fashion sense!

Au contraire!

ATOMIC VOGUE
What to wear if you're oxygen!
What goes with helium?
Beryllium today!

R. Chast

SUMMER REPLACEMENTS

R.Chast

THE CRAZY HOUR

Face gets wild.

Back hunches up.
("Halloween kitty")

Noisy runs after invisible things.

GALUMPH
GALUMPH

Back to normal.

R. Chast

BAD TRANSLATION

TOPIC PROCESSOR

Discuss

Hey! Does anyone remember last summer?

Rehash

Last summer was fun, hmmm?

Purée

Quite a summer, am I right?

Liquefy

That was _some_ _summer_, wasn't it?

R. Chast

NO HELP THERE

1 Ride-All-Day-Free Pass at Big Bert Funland*

* Except weekends and holidays.

1 50¢-off Any Purchase at Big Bert Burger Bungalow**

** Offer not good after 10 A.M.

1 Big Bert's Funland Souvenir Hat***

*** Sorry, only one per family

R. Chast

BOUND for BROADWAY

Ta da da da

Da ta da ta

Better get rid of these brown shoes.

R. Chast

SUMMER FUN GUIDE

	🚗 Traffic Jam	Splintery Picnic Tables	😵 Screaming Babies	Frisbee Aimed at Your Neck	$5.00 Hamburgers	Depressed Lifeguards	Unsavory Things on Bottom of Lake	Headache by 4 O'Clock
CRABBY STATE PARK	✓		✓			✓	✓	✓
BOOMERANG PARK		✓	✓	✓				✓
ROCKY BOTTOM PARK			✓	✓		✓	✓	✓
BIG NECK STATE PARK	✓				✓	✓		✓
THERMOS STATE PARK	✓	✓	✓	✓				✓
EDGY FALLS PARK	✓		✓	✓				✓
LAKE MONONUCLEOSIS			✓	✓	✓	✓	✓	✓

KEY: = TRAFFIC JAM   = SPLINTERY PICNIC TABLES 😢 = SCREAMING BABIES

 = FRISBEE AIMED AT YOUR NECK   = $5.00 HAMBURGERS

 = DEPRESSED LIFEGUARDS = UNSAVORY THINGS ON BOTTOM OF LAKE

 = HEADACHE BY 4 O'CLOCK

R. Chast

ART'S HANDMAIDENS   ART'S FLUNKIES

R. Chast

BROADWAY SPINOFFS

WHOSE APARTMENT IS IT, ANYWAY? ~ A big fight between roommates causes problems.

THE BEST LITTLE NURSING HOME IN TEXAS ~ Laughs abound as patients write, produce, and act in plays.

I'M NOT MISBEHAVING ~ Boy stands wrongly accused by his nanny in this searing drama.

R. Chast

COOKIE COMPARISON

Tough

PERPETUA-
CHEWS

Tougher

24
TAR BARS

Toughest

CONCRETOS

R. Chast

IN A QUANDARY

The Voice of Reason: It's not such a big thing; just put the galoshes on.

The Voice of Conscience: Mom will be mad if you don't put them on.

The Voice of Practicality: It's raining. Why don't you just wear 'em?

The Voice of Binky: Toss them out of the window.

R. Chast

HERMIT STARTER SET

1 Hammer (to smash phone, etc.)

2 Hermit All-Purpose Outfits (identical)

1 Book ("So You Want to Be a Hermit")

Fred's
SO YOU WANT
TO BE A
HERMIT

R. Chast

LOTSA DUCKS
Sure are a lotta ducks!
Maybe they're geese!
Certainly seem to be tons of 'em, no matter what!
One heckuva lot!
Gee Whillikers!
Some buncha ducks!
R. Chast

HELL'S BELLS

R. Chast

Just Asking

Q: Can electricity "leak out" of sockets?

Q: Can moisture in the air get into sockets and cause a room to become "charged"?

Q: Has ball lightning ever entered an apartment on West End Avenue?

R. Chast

HECKSAPOPPIN'

Bird's lost again!

Anybody seen Tweeter?

Jim comes over to borrow a shovel!!

Mom's cookin' burgers!!!

Dad's tie doesn't look right!!!!

Honey?

Nobody's answering the telephone !!!!!

R-R-RING

R. Chast

IN YESTERYEAR

Back when we were small, we lived on a farm about 15 miles outside Welmet, Kansas.

We were so small then! Tiny, tiny, tiny!

To keep us out of harm's way, Grandmother would place us in the cookie jar.

It was our very favorite spot in the world. The odor of Grandmother's fresh-baked treats delighted us to no end.

Sometimes, we'd even break off a crumb or two to munch on.

> Oatmeal!

The only sad part was wondering what was going on "out there."

> I think she's vacuuming.

When we got big, Grandmother threw us a party.

We still daydream about the era of the cookie jar, but as the years pass, our memories of it become fainter and fainter...

Even Grandmother can't remember it all that well.

> I'm sorry, dear, I just don't have the faintest idea what you're talking about!

R. Chast

OTHER WITCHES

The Wicked Witch of the Northeast

No more rent control!! The sky's the limit!!

The Wicked Witch of the Midwest

Ha, ha! Another huge corn surplus!

The Wicked Witch of the Sun Belt

How'd you like a 30-acre mall right in your BACK YARD, my pretty??!

R. Chast

SUIT YOURSELF

The Classical Version

The Pop Version

The Muzak Version

Enter the
LUCKY DAY
Sweepstakes!

1 GRAND PRIZE $1,000,000!	**2** FIRST PRIZES $100,000 each!	**5** SECOND PRIZES $1,000 each!	**10** THIRD PRIZES $500 each!

20 FOURTH PRIZES $100 each!	**100** FIFTH PRIZES $10 each!	**500** SIXTH PRIZES $1.00 each!	**1,000** SEVENTH PRIZES 25¢ each!

5,000 EIGHTH PRIZES 10¢ each!	**50,000** NINTH PRIZES 5¢ each!	**100,000** TENTH PRIZES 1¢ each!	**1,000,000** ELEVENTH PRIZES stamp worth 1/10¢, each!

10,000,000 TWELFTH PRIZES booklet to put above stamp into, each!	**100,000,000** THIRTEENTH PRIZES coupon to send away for booklet for stamps, each!	**1,000,000,000** FOURTEENTH PRIZES ad for company that makes booklet and stamps, not including coupon, each!	**3,000,000,000** FIFTEENTH PRIZES piece of paper bearing first initial of said company, each!

R. Chast

RAISONS d'AVOIR

Some stuff you need.

Most people do.

We're going on a spree right now!

For the heck of it.

It can't be helped, even if you're a cat.

VARIOUS BOWLS

CATNIP MOUSE

SCRATCH POST

R. Chast

ATTACK OF THE

YOUNG PROFESSIONALS!

Watch in horror as they...

...turn your neighborhood into an overpriced, high-rent boutiqueland!

...talk about their investments right in front of your eyes!

Merrill Lynch says oxen, mung beans, and rare key chains.

...dress for success even while sleeping!

WRONG   RIGHT

R. Chast

KITSCH IN NATURE

Peacocks

Any snowfall between December 22-28

The "foliage" season

R. Chast

IT'S A LIFE

Born on the right side of the tracks

Born on the wrong side of the tracks

Born on the train

R. Chast

TOO CUTE FOR COMFORT

Meow?

R. Chast

PERFECT MASTERS
FIGHT IT OUT

Who has the most Rolls-Royces? The cutest disciples?
The longest beard? The nicest swimming pool? The best
lawyers? The biggest landholdings? The spiffiest outfit?

Baba Rerodas   Subi Mumwaht   Master Shecky   Neëns En

R. Chast

LITTLE BEVERLY CARDS

  SAVE 'EM • COLLECT 'EM • TRADE 'EM

\#792
Little Beverly
stares off
into space.

\#876
Little Beverly
contemplates
getting a cold.

\#1101
Little Beverly
experiences
free-floating
anxiety.

R. Chast

Dreams of Glory

Subway seats padded in velvet; marble floors; silk-screened wallpaper.

Public phones made of the finest porcelain, studded with various jewels, and paired with comfortable recliners.

"Honor system" economy.

How much would you like to pay for this place?

R. Chast

TUESDAY NIGHT FEVER

R. Chast

THE FRIENDS CATALOGUE

Tired of your old friends? Need some new ones?
If you want all new friends, or just a couple of replacements,
SEE BELOW.

Friends #63621: Very charming
middle-aged couple

Friend #84506: Girl in arts

Friend #50139: Rambunctious boy

Friends #10296: Special
"Friends" blend

R. Chast

Uneducated Guesses

It's a RATIONAL, RATIONAL, RATIONAL, RATIONAL WORLD
Gravity's great!
You can't change the past!
What the heck's a "mood"?
If those shoes are on sale, I'll buy'em!
I've got five minutes to make my appointment!
Ghosts? That's silly!
I like Tod because he's kind and thrifty!
Two and two are four! That's the way it goes!
Things just don't go flying off into space!
Hair grows back!
R. Chast

HELP WANTED

GAL FRIDAY: Can you play with cat, eat cookies, talk on phone, read? Starting at 2539 K.

M or F needed to spend money as if it were water. $9750 wk.

OPP'TY of a lifetime: Lie on beach, watch waves. Salary up to you.

R. Chast

STRANGE PROVERBS

The ketchup of sorrow
is better than
the mustard of happiness.

Three shoes do not
a hat make.

A couch is as
good as a chair.

A song in time is
worth a dime.

Hop before
you skip.

R. Chast

WARNING SIGNS

The Telltale "n"

MILLS, REED, HADLEY 'n' RAY
LAW OFFICES

Photographs of famous clients in waiting room

Laura Dern
Love you Stephani
Thank you Barbara
HANK Larry Bob

Odd "specials"

TODAY ONLY!
FREE WITH EVERY CIVIL SUIT — 2 QUARTS OF Fred's Best ICE CREAM!

R. Chast

RECALL OF THE WILD

This one's broken.

This one's going to break any minute.

This one never worked right to begin with.

R. Chast

Our Friend, The Chickpea

The chickpea— Nature's boon to salad.

But how much do we really know about this humble edible?

We know it always shows up at salad bars, near the beets.

We know it played almost no role in World War II.

ALLIES

AXIS

CHICKPEA

Then again, neither did Sweden.

No one would call it the champagne of canned vegetables.

Even very primitive peoples have never mythologized them.

This is just a chickpea

So, what _is_ it about the chickpea that keeps us guessing?

Perhaps you ought to dial the Chickpea Hotline and find out.

R. Chast

 SILLY CHART
OF *TINA B.*

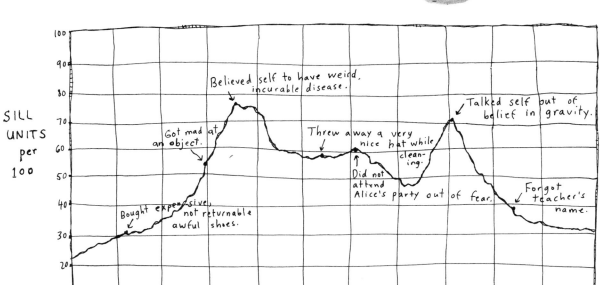

SILL UNITS per 100

Bought expensive, not returnable awful shoes.

Got mad at an object.

Believed self to have weird, incurable disease.

Threw away a very nice hat while cleaning.

Did not attend Alice's party out of fear.

Talked self out of belief in gravity.

Forgot teacher's name.

JAN. FEB. MAR. APR. MAY JUNE JULY AUG. SEPT. OCT. NOV. DEC.

R. Chast

THE FIVE "W"s

Who? The Quatorze Sisters.

Mimi Patti Elvira

What? Ate mints.

Where? On the premises.

When? Yesterday.

29 OCTOBER
ate mints.

Why? Go ask.

R. Chast

FROM BAD TO WORSE

Plastic rainhats.

Plastic rainhats that fold up in packets.

Plastic rainhats in packets that have a bank's name on them.

SHADY SAVINGS BANK
AND LOAN

Aforementioned item given as a "gift" to someone

I'd like you to have this!

R. Chast

OP-ED PAGE

BOB'S SPACE
WITH BOB LEEDS

"Sometimes things are great... and sometimes they're not so great! Or so they say!"

A WORD WITH Sheila
BY SHEILA ANDREW

"If everybody would just sit down and have a cup of tea, the world would be a much better place!"

MY LITTLE WORLD
BY GARY OAKES

"I get too much homework, but other than that, it's really not all that bad."

SOUND OFF
WITH ERIC HETS

"Last week was a better all-around week, but this week had its high points."

Millieville
WITH MILLIE COBBLER

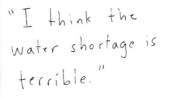

"I think the water shortage is terrible."

FROM MY EYES
BY FLUFFY

"Chicken is better than liver, but steak is better than chicken."

R. Chast

FAILURES

THE CAR

THE FAMILY

APRIL 23

Farmer's Almanac

Probably a good day to plant some string beans. Perhaps a little rain in the evening.

Dry Cleaner's Almanac

Winter coats keep pouring in. However, a cool spring makes for a lot of woollen sweater traffic.

Bump-on-a-Log's Almanac

There may be something decent on Channel 3 tonight.

R. Chast

Here They Are

The Flanders Sisters

Martina

and Polly.

They were like Night and Day.

Actually, they were more like 2 o'clock

and 4 o'clock.

R. Chast

COLLECTOR'S ITEMS

Barbie Real ~ Teenage doll comes complete with acne, weight problem, and tacky wardrobe.

Phobic Barbie ~ The doll that never leaves her packing case.

Conceptual Barbie ~ A small book of essays by various people on the idea of Barbie.

R. Chast

YOUR HONEST OPINION

SINGER OR SONG STYLIST?

WRITER OR PROSE STYLIST?

CHEF OR FOOD STYLIST?

COMPUTER PROGRAMMER OR DATA STYLIST?

R. Chast

EXTREMELY
SECRET AGENTS

Agent 77665

Agent 29

Agent 400006

Agent 12

R. Chast

Underutilized Ice-Breakers

R. Chast

RECENTLY DISCOVERED INTERNAL ORGANS

R. Chast

FAVORITE
WATER DRINKS

H₂O Punch

2 c. tap water

2 c. well water

1 c. bottled spring water

1 c. distilled water

Place ingredients in blender. Mix well.

Serves 6-8.

Alaska

Place 1 qt. water* in refrigerator for 2-4 hours. Serve immediately.

Makes 4 portions.

*any kind

Water Spritzer

Pour 2 oz. of distilled or bottled spring water in a glass over ice. Fill with club soda.

Make Mine Water

1 c. tap water

Decorate with tiny umbrella. Serves 1.

R Chast

TINY CLAIMS COURT

Neighbor's dog chewed pencil.

Flapjack mix from Dalemart bought by N.M. was spoiled.

While sewing at T.F.'s house, claimant pricked self with borrowed needle.

SO THEY SAY

Life is just a bowl of cereal!

Life is just a bowl of M&M's!

Life is just a bowl.

FACING THE FACTS

The Easter bunny? No such thing.

Santa? Totally a myth.

Astrology? Fun, maybe something to say, but mostly a bunch of baloney.

The Moon

WHAT IS YOUR SUN?

YOU and the Stars

All that's left is Ernie, and three o'clock snacks.

R. Chast

"STAR WARS": THE FINAL INSTALLMENT

Everyone in "Star Wars" and everyone in "Star Trek" winds up being related,

UNCLE KIRK !!!

except for Princess Leia, who is ultimately revealed to be an android.

In the very last scene, it all turns out to be some kid's nightmare.

R. Chast